THE ULTIMATE
HOCKEY
FACT BOOK

FOR KIDS

D1519178

Broadwood Press are an independent publishing team that aims to provide fun and educational books for young readers.

All facts within this book are accurate at the time of publishing. However, if you happen to spot anything that needs to be corrected, please email us at **broadwoodpress@gmail.com** and we will be more than happy to help you out.

ISBN: 9798863613369

1.

A form of hockey can be traced back to a game played in ancient Egypt over 4,000 years ago.

2.

The first reference to hockey in print came from an English book called Juvenile Sports and Pastime from 1773.

3.

The first recorded death in hockey came in 1842 when players fell through a frozen canal during play.

4.

The earliest known photograph of a hockey game dates back to 1881.

5.
British soldiers brought ice hockey to North America, where it became a popular sport during the long and harsh winters.

6.
Canada won the first hockey world championships at the Winter Olympics in Antwerp.

7.
Before the introduction of curved sticks, players would play with flat paddles.

8.
Hockey players can lose as much as 10 pounds of water during an NHL game.

9.
According to legend, the first hockey pucks were made from frozen cow dung.

10.
The NHL was founded in 1917 with four teams: the Montreal Wanderers, Montreal Canadiens, Toronto Arenas, and Ottawa Senators.

11.
The first US expansion team was the Boston Bruins in 1924.

12.
The first expansion team in Canada was the Montreal Maroons in 1924.

13.

Taffy Abel was the first Indigenous player to play in the NHL, suiting up for the upstart New York Rangers in 1926.

14.

The first Asian player to play in the NHL was Larry Kwan, who suited up for the Rangers in 1958.

15.

The first black player, Will O'Ree, suited up for the Boston Bruins in 1958.

16.

Wayne Gretzky holds more than 60 NHL records, more than any other NHL player.

17.

The highest-scoring brother tandem in the NHL is the Gretzky's. Wayne had 2,857 points, while his brother Brent had 4 in his NHL career.

18.

The Sutter family are the highest-scoring brothers, who combined, put up 2,934 points between the six of them.

19.

The first expansion post-original six was in 1967, with the NHL doubling to 12 teams.

20.

The NHL had its second expansion in 1970, adding the Vancouver Canucks and Buffalo Sabres.

21.

Official NHL pucks come from a single company and are kept in a freezer to prevent bouncing.

22.

The first NHL All-Star game was held in 1934 to benefit Ace Bailey, who had a career-ending injury via a hit from the infamous Eddie Shore.

23.

The original six era started in 1942 and lasted 25 years.

24.

Before the original six era, the Stanley Cup was a challenge trophy where other leagues could play for the cup.

25.

The first person to score a hat trick in the NHL was Harry "Punch" Broadbent, scoring three goals for the Ottawa Senators on December 22, 1917.

26.

Roger Neilson is responsible for three NHL rule changes, including when a goalie is pulled, the goaltender cannot leave his stick to guard the net.

27.

The original Stanley Cup was only seven inches tall. Today, the Stanley Cup is over three feet and continues to grow.

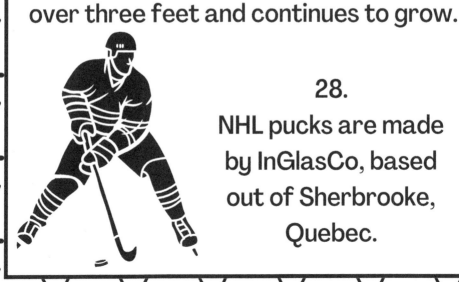

28.

NHL pucks are made by InGlasCo, based out of Sherbrooke, Quebec.

29.

The Pittsburgh Penguins had a live mascot named Penguin Pete in the late 1960s, who was on loan from the Pittsburgh Zoo.

30.

The San Jose Sharks were almost named the Blades but, due to gang implications, were eventually named the Sharks.

31.

Other names in the running included the Rubber Puckies and Screaming Squids.

32.

In the 1974 draft, the Buffalo Sabres drafted a fictitious player as a form of protest during a relatively slow draft.

33.

The Montreal Canadiens 1956 team has more than 10 players in the Hockey Hall of Fame.

34.

Jacque Plante was the first NHL goalie to wear a modern-day mask in 1959.

35.

The Penguins were the first NHL team to include last names on their jerseys in 1970.

36.

The Edmonton Oilers were the first team to retire a number. They retired Wayne Gretzky's number 99.

37.

A woman has never played in a regular-season NHL game. However, women have played exhibition games and participated in the NHL All-Star Game.

38.

Each NHL team has an affiliated AHL and ECHL team as part of their farm system.

39.

NHL players can have one-way or two-way contracts, which impact whether a player can move between the NHL and AHL.

40.

Any player on the team can be named captain, but only skaters can wear the C on their jerseys.

41.

Roberto Luongo was the first goalie in NHL history to wear the C on his mask.

42.

Each player, staff and front office staff gets a day with the Stanley Cup when their team wins.

43.

The keeper of the cup travels with the Stanley Cup and spends his summers travelling the world.

44.

After the 1994 Stanley Cup finals, the cup was found at the bottom of a hotel pool where players from the New York Rangers stayed.

45.

The last Canadian team to win the Stanley Cup was the Montreal Canadiens in 1993.

46.

There arc currently more than ten NHL franchises without a Stanley Cup.

47.

Five teams have never been to the Stanley Cup finals.

48.

The Stanley Cup has been stolen twice in its long history. The first happened in 1970, and the second in 2018.

49.

The Stanley Cup is named after Lord Stanley, who donated the trophy to be awarded to the most outstanding Canadian team.

50.

The first winner of the Stanley Cup was the Montreal Amateur Athletic Association.

51.

The Stanley Cup was initially a challenge cup with amateur teams competing.

52.

The Vancouver Millionaires Denman Arena was Canada's first artificial ice surface.

53.

The first overseas game by NHL teams was in 1938 when the Montreal Canadiens took on the Detroit Red Wings.

54.

The first recorded indoor hockey game was played at the Victoria Skating Rink in Montreal in 1875.

55.

Surprisingly, the first NHL game played outdoors was in 2003 between the Edmonton Oilers and Montreal Canadiens.

56.

The largest indoor NHL game was between the Vancouver Canucks and Ottawa Senators at BC Place Stadium.

57.

NHL teams have now played in Europe, Asia, and Oceania as part of exhibition or regular season games.

58.

The only year the Stanley Cup was not awarded was 1919 due to the Spanish Flu outbreak.

59.

The official rink dimensions of NHL rinks are 200 feet long and 85 feet wide.

60.

The first recorded women's ice hockey game occurred in Ottawa, Canada, in 1892.

61.

The Hart Memorial Trophy is awarded annually to the player judged most valuable to his team.

62.

The Lady Byng Memorial Trophy is awarded to a player with outstanding sportsmanship and is typically awarded to players with low penalty minutes.

63.

The Vezina Trophy is awarded to the league's top goaltender.

64.

The Calder Memorial Trophy is awarded to the NHL's rookie of the year, with certain restrictions.

65.

The Art Ross Trophy is awarded to the player who leads the league in total points at the end of the regular season.

66.

The James Norris Memorial trophy is awarded to the top defencemen of the year.

67.

The Bill Masterton Memorial Trophy is awarded to a player who showcases perseverance, sportsmanship, and dedication to hockey.

68.

The Ted Lindsey Award is given to the NHL player selected as the most outstanding by the NHL Players Association members.

69.

The Jack Adams Award is given to the coach of the Year.

70.

The Frank J. Selke trophy is awarded to the forward who shows exemplary skills as a defensive forward.

71.

The Williams M. Jennings Award goes to the goalie with the fewest goals conceded in the regular season with a minimum of 25 starts.

72.

The King Clancy Award is awarded to a player who has made a noteworthy humanitarian contribution to their community.

73.
Fighting is a part of the game in the NHL, and worthy combatants receive a 5-minute major penalty for fighting.

74.
The only long-term breaks in NHL games are the two commercial breaks per period.

75.
The NHL's tallest player ever was Zdeno Chara, who was 6 foot 9 inches.

76.
Phil Kessel holds the 'Iron Man of the NHL' with 1064 games played in a row.

77.

The Maurice "Rocket" Richard trophy is awarded to the leading goal scorer in the NHL.

78.

The Mark Messier Leadership Award is awarded to a player who exemplifies outstanding leadership during the regular season.

79.

The Jim Gregory General Manager of the Year is an annual award given to the top General Manager.

80.

The Yakuza most likely owned the Tampa Bay Lightning at one point in their history.

81.

The E.J. McGuire Award of Excellence is given to a draft prospect who best exemplifies excellence through character, competitiveness, and athleticism.

82.

A member of the British Royal Family once defrauded the Tampa Bay Lightning.

83.

The Tampa Bay Lightning held the attendance record for the NHL until the first outdoor game.

84.

No player drafted by the Tampa Bay Lightning had won the Stanley Cup until Brad Richards won in 2015.

85.
At one point, Tampa Bay had their nets, pucks and team sticks confiscated as part of a lawsuit loss.

86.
Manon Rheaume became the first woman to play in the NHL when she appeared in an exhibition game for the Tampa Bay Lightning.

87.
The location of the Columbus Blue Jackets stadium is a former prison site.

88.
After every goal, the Columbus Blue Jackets shoot a replica cannon off.

89.

The Columbus Blue Jackets had the first Finnish General Manager in the NHL.

90.

The Columbus Blue Jackets are one of two teams to never appear in a conference final.

91.

The Blue Jackets are named after Ohio's Civil War history.

92.

Sidney Crosby scored the golden goal in 2010, securing Canada the gold medal at the Vancouver Olympics.

93.

The Colorado Avalanche were the first team to win a Stanley Cup in their first season after relocation.

94.

The Colorado Avalanche relocated from Quebec City in 1995.

95.

Patrick Roy won the Stanley Cup in 1986 with the Montreal Canadiens, in 1996 with the Colorado Avalanche, and the Memorial Cup as a coach with the Quebec Ramparts.

96.

The Colorado Avalanche were almost called the Rocky Mountain Extreme.

97.

The Colorado Avalanche were the first team to win a Stanley Cup the same year they hosted their first NHL All-Star Game.

98.

The Boston Bruins hold the record for most short-handed goals during a single penalty.

99.

The Boston Bruins have won six Stanley Cups in their history.

100.

Zdeno Chara holds the record for the hardest shot in the NHL. He registered a 108.8 mph shot at the 2012 NHL All-Star Skills Competition.

101.

More than fifty players and seven staff members from the Boston Bruins are in the Hockey Hall of Fame.

102.

The Bruin's Pat McReavy had his name spelt wrong on the Stanley Cup when the Bruins won in 1941.

103.

When the replica cup was made in 1957, his name was corrected.

104.

The Anaheim Ducks were initially named the Mighty Ducks of Anaheim after their Disney links.

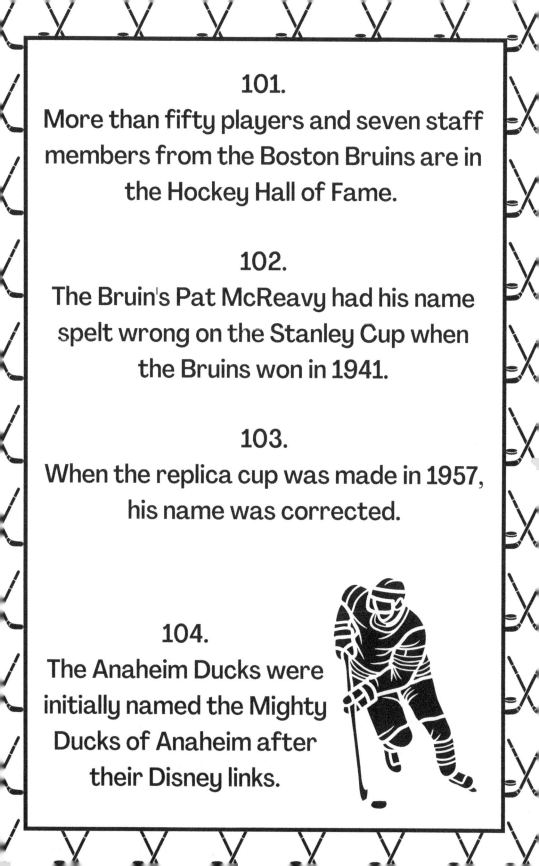

105.

As part of their sale from Disney, the Ducks rebranded with a new color pallet of orange, black and gold.

106.

The Ducks mascot is named Wild Wing.

107.

The Ducks won the Stanley Cup in 2007 when they beat the Ottawa Senators in five games.

108.

The Ducks Jean-Sebastien Giguere won the Conn Smythe Trophy as the playoff MVP in 2003, despite losing.

109.

The Chicago Blackhawks have the only goalie inscribed on the Stanley Cup as captain.

110.

The Arizona Coyotes currently play in the smallest NHL rink. The team uses Arizona State University's Mullett Arena, which seats 4,600 people.

111.

The Coyotes were relocated in 1996 from Winnipeg .

112.

The Arizona Coyotes changed their name from the Phoenix Coyotes to better market themselves to the broader state.

113.

Three Native American tribes approved the Arizona Coyote's kachina logo.

114.

Other names from the Phoenix Coyotes included Outlaws, Mustangs, Wranglers, and Freeze.

115.

The initial owners of the Phoenix Coyotes also owned the Phoenix Suns.

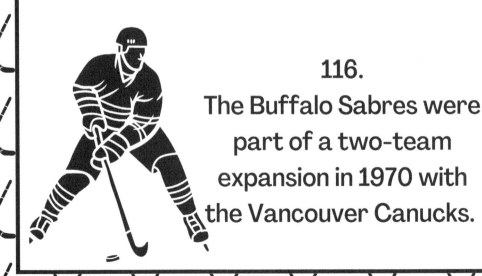

116.

The Buffalo Sabres were part of a two-team expansion in 1970 with the Vancouver Canucks.

117.

Both the Sabres and the Vancouver Canucks have not won a Stanley Cup.

118.

Then-owner Seymour Knox named the Sabres after the sabre, a weapon carried by a leader.

119.

The Sabres made the Stanley Cup finals in their fifth year and lost to the Philadelphia Flyers in six games.

120.

That playoff series had the infamous fog game where the game was played in heavy fog.

121.

The Sabres have undergone a few jersey changes but eventually returned to their royal blue and gold look.

122.

The infamous 'banana slug' occasionally does make an appearance as their third jersey.

123.

The Calgary Flames were relocated from Atlanta.

124.

The Flames play in the worst-ranked stadium, the Scotiabank Saddledome.

125.
The Flames mascot is Harvey the Hound.

126.
Calgary and Edmonton have a fierce rivalry called the Battle of Alberta.

127.
The Carolina Hurricanes have enjoyed several viral videos after victories with various dances and antics.

128.
The Canes still own the Whalers IP and have used the iconic Whalers jerseys as a one-off jersey several times.

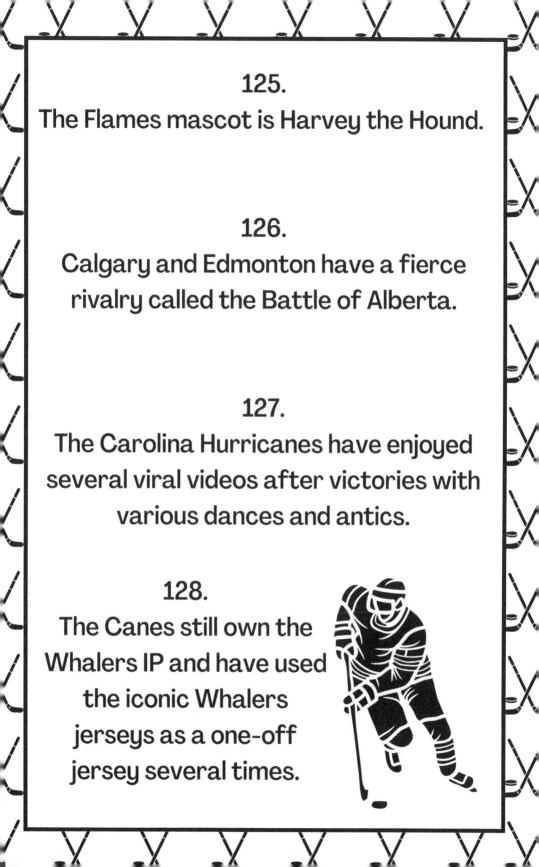

129.

Carolina Hurricane fans are called Caneiacs.

130.

The Hurricanes were a relocation of the beloved Hartford Whalers.

131.

The Canes won their first Stanley Cup in 2006 but missed the playoffs the following year.

132.

The Chicago Blackhawks are named after the infamous Blackhawk regiment of the US Army.

133.
Although officially called the United Center, the Blackhawk fans refer to their arena as the Madhouse on Madison.

134.
Connor Bedard was the first-ever super underager in the Western Hockey League.

135.
The Chicago Blackhawks have come under fire from activists for using Native American imagery for their logo.

136.
The Detroit Red Wings and Montreal Maroons played the longest game in NHL history.

137.
The game ended 1-0 after 116 minutes and 30 seconds of overtime.

138.
Pavel Datsuk of the Detroit Red Wings never had a regular season hat-trick.

139.
Ted Lindsey started the victory lap tradition with the Stanley Cup after the Red Wings 1950 Stanley Cup win.

140.
The Red Wings participated in an outdoor game in 1954 against prisoners at Marquette Branch Prison.

141.

Marguerite Norris was the first woman with her name on the Stanley Cup. She was the President of the Detroit Red Wings in 1954.

142.

Detroit Red Wing fans throw an octopus on the ice before the playoffs.

143.

The Detroit Red Wings hold the longest consecutive playoff appearance streak.

144.

The Ottawa Senator's Daniel Alfredson scored the first NHL regular season shootout goal.

145.

The Ottawa Senators are among the only teams in history to make the Stanley Cup finals without a single shutout in the regular season.

146.

Elgin Street in Ottawa is renamed the Red Mile when the team is in the playoffs.

147.

The Ottawa Senators play in Kanata, Ontario, about 45 minutes from downtown Ottawa.

148.

The Ottawa Senators and Vancouver Canucks played in the NHL's only outdoor regular season game held indoors.

149.

The Montreal Canadiens' former home, the Montreal Forum, is now a movie theatre and shopping center.

150.

The Canadiens are the most famous hockey franchises in Canada and are nicknamed the Habs.

151.

The Postal Code for the Bell Centre is H4B 5Go or HABS GO!

152.

Montreal and Ottawa are the only two NHL cities that sing the Canadian national anthem in French and English.

153.

The Canadiens pre-game torch ceremony is always performed by a local minor hockey player.

154.

The Washington Capitals hold the record for the worst record in the NHL, with only 21 points in 1974-75.

155.

That Washington Capitals 74-75 team also had a -265 differential and a single win on the road.

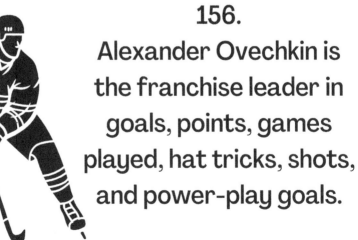

156.

Alexander Ovechkin is the franchise leader in goals, points, games played, hat tricks, shots, and power-play goals.

157.

The Vegas Golden Knights were the first expansion team in the 2010s and started play in 2017.

158.

After other expansion drafts left teams at the bottom of the standings, the NHL changed the rules to give Vegas a better chance for success.

159.

The Golden Knights won their first Stanley Cup in 2023 with a five-game defeat of the Florida Panthers.

160.

The Golden Knights are known for having some of the best in-game experiences.

161.
They have a drum line, acrobats, and a host of big Vegas acts coming through and entertaining the fans.

162.
The Winnipeg Jets is the second iteration of the Jets, with the original jets moving to Phoenix in the 90s.

163.
The Jets 2.0 was a relocation of the Atlanta Thrashers, who struggled for attendance during their brief existence.

164.
The current goal-scoring leader for the Jets is Ilya Kovalchuk, who never played a game in Winnipeg.

165.

The Winnipeg Jets Canada Life Centre is the second smallest stadium in the NHL. It's only bigger than the Arizona Coyotes Mullett Arena.

166.

The Dallas Star's Brett Hall became part of the first father-son tandem to enter the Hockey Hall of Fame in 2009.

167.

The Stars considered renaming the team when they moved to Dallas.

168.

Originally founded as the Minnesota North Stars, the Dallas Stars kept the same branding and colors as their former team.

169.

The Stars play at the American Airlines Center and have one of the top fan experiences in the NHL.

170.

Celena Rae is the official anthem singer of the Dallas Stars.

171.

She is also a former semi-finalist on American Idol.

172.

The Edmonton Oilers were part of the World Hockey Association before joining the NHL.

173.

The Oilers won two WHA championships during its tenure.

174.

The Oilers and Edmonton Elk's success in the 1980s led the city of Edmonton becoming known as 'the City of Champions'.

175.

The 1983-84 Edmonton Oilers set the NHL record for most goals scored by a team (446) and fewest goals allowed (226).

176.

That same 1983-84 year, Wayne Gretzky put up a 215-point season.

177.

Former Edmonton Oilers player Mark Messier holds the NHL record for the most playoff game-winning goals in a career.

178.

The Florida Panthers fans throw plastic rats on the ice during playoff games.

179.

The Panthers were originally going to be in Miami, but owner Wayne Huizenga opted to locate the team in Sunrise, Florida.

180.

The Panthers have made two Stanley Cup Finals but have never won the cup.

181.

The Panthers are named after the endangered Florida Panther.

182.

While playing for the Florida Panthers, Jaromir Jagr scored 1,888 points.

183.

The Los Angeles Kings were one of the first expansion teams in 1967. They joined a fellow California team, the California Seals, in the league.

184.

The Kings refer to the ultras as the King's Court and have numerous LA-based celebrity fans.

185.
The Kings play in the Crypto.com Arena.

186.
They are the fourth team to play there with the other three being the Sparks, Lakers, and Clippers.

187.
The Kings mascot is named Bailey, who is a lion.

188.
Wayne Gretzky was traded to LA in 1988 and would go on to cement hockey in the broader US market.

189.
The Minnesota Wild logo is a silhouette of a bear.

190.
The official colours of the Minnesota Wild are forest green, iron range red, Minnesota wheat and harvest gold.

191.
After a hat trick, hockey fans traditionally throw their hat on the ice.

192.
Minnesota is known as the 'State of Hockey' and has an annual high school tournament based out of the Wild's rink every year.

193.

The official fight song of the Wild is "Let's Go Crazy" by Prince.

194.

The Nashville Predators were an expansion team when they joined the league in 1998.

195.

The Nashville Predator's mascot is a saber-tooth tiger.

196.

Chris Mason is the second goalie in history to have a goal in both the AHL and NHL.

197.

Scott Stevens number 4 was the first number the New Jersey Devils retired.

198.

Patrik Sundstrom holds the playoff record of eight points in a Devils 10-4 victory over the Washington Capitals in a single game.

199.

Martin Brodeur played in New Jersey for 21 straight seasons.

200.

In 1985, Pat Verbeek cut off his thumb in the offseason in a farming accident... Ouch!!

201.

The Islanders won four consecutive Stanley Cup championships between 1980-83.

202.

They were also the first NHL team to win a Stanley Cup with Europeans on the roster.

203.

Mike Bossy scored 50 goals in 50 games in 1981 for the New York Islanders.

204.

The New York Islanders were once bought by a fraudster, John Spano, who faked his net worth.

205.

The Islanders' UBS Arena replaced its traditional home, the Nassau Veteran Memorial Coliseum, in 2021.

206.

Mark Messier famously guaranteed the Rangers would win Game 7 of the 1994 Stanley Cup finals... they did.

207.

Their 1994 Stanley Cup win broke a 54-year cup drought.

208.

Mark Messier was the first player to captain two different franchises, the Oilers, and Rangers, to a cup win.

209.
The last New York Ranger to wear the number nine was Pavel Bure.

210.
In the history of the NHL, a New York Ranger has only won the scoring title three times.

211.
Brian Leetch was the first non-Canadian to win the Conn Smythe Trophy during the 1994 Stanley Cup title run.

212.
The Philadelphia Flyers teams in the 1970s were known as the Broadstreet Bullies.

213.
The Flyer's Gritty is one of the NHL's most famous mascots.

214.
The Flyers have struggled to find an identity post-NHL lockout and continue re-tooling.

215.
Since 1999, the Flyers have used more than 17 goalies, an NHL record.

216.
Mark Recchi holds the single-season point lead for the Flyers with 123 points in the 1992-93 season.

217.

The San Jose Sharks once had to cancel a game due to flooding at their arena.

218.

Sharks staff once found a stray black cat and named it "Pawvelski".

219.

Patrick Marleau's family ended up adopting the lucky cat.

220.

The Sharks have over 100 palm trees lining their arena walk-up area.

221.

The Sharks skate through a giant shark head for their entrance.

222.

The Shark's first home stadium was the 'Cow Palace'.

223.

The Seattle Kraken joined the NHL in the 2021 - 2022 season.

224.

The team plays in Climate Pledge Arena, home to the Seattle Supersonics.

225.

The Kraken are the second pro team to play in the city.

226.

The first was the Seattle Metropolitans of the Pacific Coast Hockey League.

227.

The Kraken's team name was chosen via fan engagement. It was one of 1,200 names submitted.

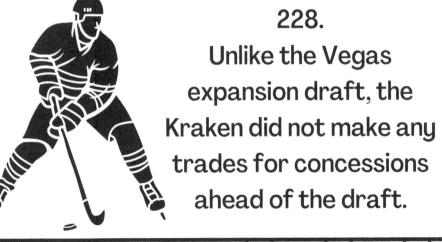

228.

Unlike the Vegas expansion draft, the Kraken did not make any trades for concessions ahead of the draft.

229.

The Blues are named after the music genre as former owner Sid Saloman Jr. said, "No matter where you go, there's singing. That's the spirit of St Louis".

230.

The Blues made the Stanley Cup final in their first season in 1968.

231.

David Backes of the Blues has a pilot's licence.

232.

No 2019 Stanley Cup-winning Blues team player had ever won a cup in their careers.

233.

The Blues were the fourth team in history to win three straight road games in the Stanley Cup finals.

234.

The Toronto Maple Leafs currently have the longest-running Stanley Cup drought. They last won in 1967.

235.

In the 1920s, the Toronto Maple Leafs had the same coach, Mike Rodden, as the CFL's Toronto Argonauts.

236.

The Leaf's only goalie captain was John Ross Roach in the 1924-25 season.

237.
Kevin Maguire is the only Maple Leafs player to also ref in the NHL.

238.
Bobby Orr played a single game as a Toronto Marlie in 1965. He played on loan from the Oshawa Generals.

239.
Maple Leafs Garden, the previous home of the Maple Leafs, is now a smaller university rink and a grocery store.

240.
Conn Smythe designed the Maple Leaf's logo while also the team's owner, general manager, and coach.

241.
The Leafs have the largest fan base in Canada and play every Saturday night as the 7 p.m. EST game.

242.
Justin Beiber and Drake are both big Maple Leaf fans.

243.
The Vancouver Canucks have never played the Pittsburgh Penguins in the playoffs.

244.
Ex-Vancouver Canuck Gino Odjick had the most penalty minutes in the NHL in the 20th century.

245.

There have been more than four sets of twins in the NHL.

246.

Of these, Vancouver's Daniel and Henrik Sedin were the most successful.

247.

The Vancouver Canucks played in the Western Hockey League before joining the NHL in 1970.

248.

The Canucks are named after the wartime comic book character Johnny Canuck.

249.

The Canucks mascot is Fin the Orca

250.

When twins Henrik and Daniel Sedin were first introduced to the media, they switched jerseys.

251.

The IIHF (International Ice Hockey Federation) is headquartered in Zurich, Switzerland.

252.

There are more than 80 member nations of the IHHF.

253.

Czechoslovakia beat Austria 21-4 at the 1981 World Junior Championships.

254.

That's also the most goals scored by a team in the tournament's history.

255.

Canada has won the most World Junior Hockey Championships with over 15 gold medals.

256.

Only five players have led the World Juniors and NHL in points.

257.
Phil Kessel led the 2006 World Junior Championships with 11 points, and his sister Amanda Kessell topped the u18 Women's Worlds with 19 points in 2009.

258.
The World Junior Championships are a huge deal in Canada and are given prime-time TV spots.

259.
The World Juniors cycle locations with Canada, the United States, and Europe as the cycle.

260.
The IIHF Men's World Championships are held in April every year.

261.
This time also happens to be in the middle of the NHL playoffs.

262.
European and international ice surfaces are 20 percent larger than NHL ice surfaces.

263.
The International Ice Hockey Federation was founded in 1908.

264.
The first Winter Olympic ice hockey event was held in France at the 1924 Chamonix Olympics.

265.
There are five tiers of professional hockey in North America. The NHL is at the top of the pyramid.

266.
Each league owns 51% of a player's contract, and there is no relegation or promotion.

267.
The American Hockey League is the development league for the NHL.

268.
This means most players in the league are under contract with an NHL team.

269.

The East Coast Hockey League is the tier two development league with some players under contract with an NHL team.

270.

The Southern Professional Hockey League and Federal Prospects Hockey League are the other two leagues in the pyramid.

271.

The AHL is nicknamed 'the jungle'.

272.

North American junior players generally play in the Canada Hockey League or NCAA.

273.

The CHL has three sub-leagues: the Western Hockey League, the Ontario Hockey League, and the Quebec Major Junior Hockey League.

274.

Each CHL league sends the three league champions to compete for the Memorial Cup, and the host rounds out the round-robin tournament.

275.

Each team in the CHL can have two over-age players who are 20 and below.

276.

For every year a player plays in the CHL, they are awarded a funded scholarship to attend a Canadian university.

277.

Beer league hockey is a popular recreational sport in Canada and the United States.

278.

Kunlun Red Stars are the only professional hockey team in China. They compete in the Kontinental Hockey League.

279.

The Professional Women's Hockey League was founded in 2023.

280.

The PWHL features three teams in Canada and three teams in the US with a 24-game schedule.

281.
NHL teams have an emergency backup goalie who can play for either team at every game.

282.
An emergency backup, David Ayers, beat his hometown Leafs when he played for the Carolina Hurricanes

283.
The 1980 Miracle on Ice, where the United States beat the Soviet Union, is considered one of the top sports moments of the century.

284.
The Soviet Union had one of the strongest hockey teams in international competition for much of the 20th century.

285.

80% of Canada watched the Olympic Gold Medal Game in Vancouver in 2010.

286.

Glenn Hall played in 502 consecutive games as a goalie.

287.

A team of NHL all-stars took on Soviet Union teams throughout the 1960s, 70s and 80s.

288.

The Canada Cup was an invitation-only tournament held five times in the 70s, 80s and 90s.

289.

Canada won four Canada Cup titles, with the Soviet Union winning in 1981.

290.

Canada and the Soviet Union faced off in the 1972 Summit Series. Four games were played in Canada, and four in the Soviet Union.

291.

Canada won the Summit Series with a record of 4-3-1.

292.

The Allan Cup is awarded to Canada's top senior ice hockey champions.

293.
Canada traditionally sent the Allan Cup champion to be Canada's Olympic and World Championship team.

294.
A hockey puck weighs roughly six ounces.

295.
The standard hockey puck design was officially adopted in 1885.

296.
The average NHL game uses 12 hockey pucks, with pucks going out of play being common.

297.
To help reduce spectator injuries, top leagues have mesh around the end of the rink to catch wayward pucks

298.
The last time a single puck made it through a whole game was in 1979.

299.
This puck is on display at the Hockey Hall of Fame which can be found in Toronto.

300.
NASA uses pucks to train astronauts to deal with free-floating equipment in space.